The Market Calls

A Primer on the Strategy of Writing Covered Calls

Edward Francis Doherty

Order this book online at www.trafford.com
or email orders@trafford.com

Most Trafford titles are also available at major online book retailers.

Printed in the United States of America.

ISBN: 978-1-4669-9469-0 (sc)
ISBN: 978-1-4669-9468-3 (e)

Trafford rev. 06/03/2013

 www.trafford.com

North America & international
toll-free: 1 888 232 4444 (USA & Canada)
phone: 250 383 6864 ♦ fax: 812 355 4082

Contents

Writing Covered Calls

Introduction

I *have heard it said more than once in my lifetime "Enjoy everything you do in life, because if you do not it isn't worth doing". Read this book with confidence and good intentions and you will reap enjoyment in the application.*

It is not my intent with this book to create a 100% complete and accurate manuscript for all. My intent in writing this book is to communicate with those who are both ambitious and young in spirit but are most of all patient. I have formatted this book especially for those who want to enjoy life and have fun with the Market. It is not for technical gurus or market analysts. It is for those who want an enjoyable, easy and simplistic magic carpet ride.

I believe it is the journey that is the prize, not the destination.

The application of this technique should bring substantial income to most—a rewarding amount of capital with a moderate amount of effort.

The Strategy proposed is based on reinvesting your profit and compounding the value of your investment without requiring huge amounts of money. Call your Granny right away and get the investment dollars. I'll wait.

Welcome to Covered Call Writing.

Covered call writing (selling) is a very simple method and is amazingly rewarding. What follows is a clear and concise description and examples of the technique of Covered Calls with very little emphasis on market jargon and with very few detours.

The soundness of the Covered Call process has been expounded over the years—it is a tried and true method of investing with one of the highest success rates. Whatever your background, the material presented is valuable in growing your portfolio.

Compounding, in the sense it is used here is simply reinvesting the profits and making money on the new sum. If you invest $1000 and get a 6% profit you then have $1060. If you reinvest the entire amount and get a 6% profit you now have $1,123.60. You can see how more quickly the pot can grow by reinvesting.

Consider an initial investment of $2000. If you made as little as 2% every month and reinvested that amount for twenty years you would end up with $227,000 or approximately 100 times your initial investment.

Here is your reaction!!

What? I'm no dummy. That is over 24% a year. Are you nuts?

Here is my response. Yes I am. Nuts about Covered Calls and just for that I am not going to sell you this book!

Ok! You twisted my arm. You can buy the book as long as you own a computer.

What? You don't have a computer? Run right out and get one. I'll wait.

So Granny gives you a few grand that she can spare and you can have fun with the rewards coming in at a later time. Granny won't care. Don't put any more money into the pot—just cover the calls and have some fun. That is the essence of patience!

*If you want more, and I can feel that you will, take a look now at the compounding example in Appendix B. Appendix **B** contains a print-out of a Microsoft Excel program that allows you to compute your compounded earnings for any reasonable monthly percentage. The example shows the results of compounding a gain of 3.5% a month.*

With an investment of $500 and a monthly profit of 3.5% you will net approximately $1,860,860.00 in twenty years. You will also net a nice tax problem—get it?—a NICE tax problem.

This book is about developing those skills with tried and true methods of application and using available

online trading companies such as Ameritrade, E-Trade, Scottrade etc.

Open an Account now!. Go to Chapter 4 and move on the Market. All you need is an nitial amount to establish an account—usually a few hundred dollars. While you read the rest of this book you will be able to go into your account and experience some of the information offered here.

Get in and get out of the Market. You do not want to own stock forever, and you won't be at the mercy of the Market whims. Rely on the concept of accumulating cash, acquiring capital and utilizing the art of compounding to set the pace for your future!

Money Baby! The idea is to accumulate money and enjoy spending it. That is what it is for! *You do like money—right? Money is my friend so treat it right!*

The good part is that you do not have to spend a great deal of time at this and it is nice watching your money grow without the complication of intricate stock evaluations. And yes, you should dip into the pot now and then and treat your Honey to the good life.

It is all about the Journey and the Journey starts here!

Chapter 1

Equity Call Options 101

*S*o *what is an option? What is a Call and why am I writing anything.*

Options come in several forms such as; Equity Options, Index Options, Foreign Currency Options and others. There are two types of Equity Options—Puts and Calls. To be a Covered Call expert you are only concerned with Equity Call Options.

And Yes—an Equity is a Stock.

Options have several important characteristics:

1. *Options are legal contracts with a time limit—they expire on the Saturday after the third Friday of the Month.*
2. *Equity Options are always sold in 100 share contracts*
3. *Options are leverage items*
4. *Options are RRRisky!*
5. *Options have their own Exchange*

6. *An Option is a lien on a stock and must be removed before the stock can be sold.*

1. Options are contracts with expiration dates.

*Let's suppose that you see a house that you want to buy and resell. In order to resell, the house needs fixing. You do not know what is required to make the house sell at a profit but you like the neighborhood and have sold houses in this area for much higher than the asking price. The asking price of this particular house is reasonable and you feel that with a little effort you can fix it and resell at a profit. In order to buy you time to evaluate all the costs involved you approach the present owner with a deal to give him money in exchange for the right to purchase the house three months down the road at the present asking price. You have asked for a **three month Option**. You give him $1000 as an incentive to wait the three months. A contract is drawn up. If all looks good then you exercise your option and buy the house—fix it up—and resell for a profit. The present owner keeps the $1000 no matter if you exercise your option or not.*

This is the same thing as a stock option in which the stock is the house. Like the house the stock is owned. The time limit in this case is the three months. You own the stock and sell someone the right to purchase the stock at the agreed to price for a period of time. <u>You always keep the money you get for the sale of the option.</u>

2. An option contract is always 100 shares.

*When you purchase **one contract** of a particular stock you control **100 shares** of that stock until the option expires.*

The next amount is two hundred shares or two options. This is the standard for equity options in the marketplace. If an option costs $1 per share this automatically relates to a purchase price of $100 for one contract.

The Options Market is separate from the Stock Market. We will address only a small portion of the Options market. Options can be your friend. Understand that the market makers are not always on your side but your knowledge of options and the powerful leverage (options are the poor man's market) that they afford are your ticket for ultimate success. We are talking about the ability to utilize options to provide income and offset losses when properly handled.

3. Options are leverage items

The statement "The Options Market is the poor man's Stock market" stems from the idea that the cost of an option is a fraction of the cost of the stock. If a stock is expensive—say $150 share—one cannot purchase many shares on a low budget. An option on the stock might cost $8 while the stock itself is selling for $150. To control 1000 shares of this stock with options all that is needed is $8000. To own 1000 shares you would need an investment of at least $150,000

*Notice the language. With an option you **control** the stock for a **period of time**. You do not own the stock as in a purchase. The risks are higher but if used properly one can **leverage** a large amount of stock for a reasonably low cost.*

You will learn this well when we get to the application of the Covered Call in the next chapter. Selling a call is easily attained for most stocks that have options. Not all stocks are optionable.

4. Options are RRRisky

Options expire and are inherently risky for this reason. When you Write a Covered Call you are on one of the least risky sides of options. You sell an option and wait to see the results of the underlying stock. The stock either stays the same, moves up or moves down. In all three cases the only time you stand to lose is when the stock goes down substantially. Often, even when this happens the only thing you lose is time. You still own the stock and you can sell another call, and another call and another call etc. The buyer of the call has the most risk. He stands to lose his entire investment. He wins when the stock goes up and loses when it stays the same or goes down—two out of three times. Still the chance of the big earnings is great and there is never a shortage of call buyers.

Even though you are on the least risky side of Covered Call Writing, you should know all the risks while playing with options. When you open your account with the online broker you will have access to all the information on all of the Option Exchanges and you should take advantage of this info. _There will be plenty more on this later._

5. Options have their own Exchange.

The Chicago Board of Option Exchange CBOE sets the rules and regulations for trading Options.

6. Options are a lien against a stock.

If you sell a call option on an underlying stock, the stock is actually held in a kind of escrow until the option contract is *satisfied. Satisfaction of an option is accomplished either by buying back the equivalent amount you sold or by expiration with or without assignment.*

A few definitions:

Call Option *is a contract that gives the buyer the right to <u>"call</u> the stock away" from the owner at an agreed-to price (Strike Price) and for an agreed to period.*

Covered Call *is simply selling a Call Option on stock that you own. Since you own the stock you are able to deliver it in the event that your are called out (the option buyer exercises his right to buy your stock in accordance with the option contract). In the jargon of the market maker, since you own the stock, you are* **covered.** *The Covered Call simply entails purchasing a stock that has options and selling a call option to make money.*

Strike Price *is an agreed-to (contract) price for the sale or purchase of an Option.*

Our task in the Covered Call arena is get adept at selecting the right stock and selling the right option that will provide the best premium and the most promising success. Selling the call option is your cash flow—Amen!

Example time!!!!

Yay!. This will get you to step one—appreciation! With enough examples you will be an expert.

OPTION EXAMPLE 1

We are going to look at a comparison of two simple transactions.

We will compare the simple "buy and sell" of a stock with the simple "buy and sell' of an option.

The point is to demonstrate how the purchase of an option will net, under certain conditions, a greater percentage return on investment than buying and selling the stock itself. The operative words here are Return on Investment or **ROI**.

First we look at buying and selling a stock for profit.

A. *You buy and sell XYZ stock*

For our case let's assume that the stock moves in the following fashion.

XYZ Corporation

Date	Stock.
Jan	$20
Feb	$21
Mar	$22

In January, the price of the XYZ corporation stock is $20 per share. You purchase 100 shares of the stock at a price of $2000. For this example we will include the commission costs. In future examples we will drop the commissions for clarity. Here we have two commissions since we bought and sold the stock. Let's assume the commissions are $12 for each transaction. The total cost then is $2024 for 100 shares.

The stock goes from $20 a share to $22 a share in two months—March. You sell the stock at $22 for a profit of $2 per share.

Let's take a look.

Your Rate of Return (ROI) on this transaction is **8.7%**

Total Cost	Income from Sale	Profit	%ROI
$2024	$2,200	$176	**8.7%**
			($176/$2024) x 100%

Now let's look at Buying and Selling just the Option.

B.   *Your Cousin Buys & Sells $20 March Call Options*

Let's say your cousin Vinny buys a call contract on the same stock. You don't really like your cousin so it is not surprising that you don't know what he is doing. He pays $1 per share for one hundred shares (1 contract). So his cost is $100 plus two commissions (buy and sell). Option commissions are different from stock commissions and are based on the number of options. Typically option commissions go for around $10 basic cost and an additional $1 per contract. Therefore the commission on this one contract would be approximately $11 i.e. $10 basic and $1 for each contract. For a buy and sell position, his total commission would be $22 and his total cost is $122.

The stock and the options look like this.

Date	Stock	Option Value	Time Remaining.
Jan	$20	$ 1.00	2 Months
Feb	$21	$ 1.50	1 Month
Mar	$22	$ 2.00	**Just Prior to Expiration**

So when the stock moves from $20 to $22 he earns $2 per share for 100 shares or $200. His Return on Investment is 64% because his investment was only $122.

Your Cousin's ROI

Total Cost	Income from Sale	Profit	%ROI
$122	$200	$78	64%
			($78/$122) x 100%

These are examples of stock transactions that occur in the market every day. Since the stock increased in value both you and your cousin made a profit. Look at the difference in percentage return. It is greater than 8 to 1.

<u>*This is Leverage with a big L.*</u>

What if your cousin invested as much as you did—$2000 instead of $100.

The call is $1 per share, so for $2000 plus commissions he buys 20 contracts. The option commission is $10 base fee +$1 for each contract or $30 to buy 2000 shares. He coughs up $2030 and then controls 2000 shares of the stock. <u>He does not own anything</u>.

Because the stock went up to $22 per share, he exercises his option to buy the stock at $20 a share which is the agreed to strike price.

<u>Theoretically</u> *he must buy the stock for $40,000 and take ownership of 2000 shares. Since they are now worth $22 each, he sells the 2000 shares on the market for $44,000 less commissions.*

If the stock was bought and sold for the profit, with the above examples Cuz might have to have a considerable amount of cash to buy the stock and resell it on the market. In most cases the call owner never really takes possession of the stock. What actually happens is that the option is traded directly so that he merely sells the option for the increased price—the option was bought at $1 and was sold for $2 and two commissions apply. His profit is:

Total Income	Total Cost
$4000 (2000 shares @ $2 ea.)	**$2,060** ($2000 +$60 Commission.)
Total Profit= $4000-$2,060	**$1,940**

He got $1940 for investing the same amount that you did. You got $200 for selling the stock. Notice the magnified movement in the option as compared to the stock—the stock went up by 5% and the option went up by 100%. This is Leverage! Leverage! Leverage!

How do you like your Cousin now??

Now let's put the whole thing in perspective. <u>**These examples were merely to demonstrate the Leverage power of options.**</u> The risk is very high so that if the above stock stayed the same or decreased the option would expire worthless.

We want to use the power of the covered call to give us the edge two out of three times. If the stock increases we win. If the stock stays the same we win. If the stock goes down we may win or lose depending on the severity of the decrease.

Therein lies the power of Covered Call Writing.

Since you are going to be Covered Call experts we will now do a Covered Call Write with the same stock.'

The procedure is for you to purchase the stock and for you to sell the March $20 Call for $1. Sell it to Cuz!

C. <u>You buy the stock and sell the $20 March call</u>

Your ROI:

Total Cost	Option Sale Income	Profit	%ROI
$2012	$100	$88	**4.37%**
			($88/$2012) x 100%

This is a two month ROI so the monthly return is approximately 2.18%.

Notes:

We calculate a Return on Investment by simply dividing the profit by the actual cost and multiply by 100% to obtain a percentage. This will be done throughout.

For simplicity, future examples will not include commissions.

Let's recap so that we are clear as to what actually happened step by step.

1. You owned 100 shares of stock and you sold one contract (100 shares) for $100. You had an income of $100 for selling the Call.
2. During the option period the stock went up $2— from $20 to $22.

3. You gave your cousin the right to take the stock from you at the Strike Price of $20.
4. Cuz sold his options for $2 each and raked in a net profit of $78.
5. Cuz made $78 and by investing only $122. His ROI was then 64%.
6. Your profit was $88 and your ROI was $88/$2012 or 4.37%.

*Hello! So you have 4% and Cuz has 64%. So this covered call business stinks and you are a **Dummy**. You should buy and sell calls instead.*

So now it is time for The Question!

The Question? Hey!—there is always a question.

Here it is!!

So why are we giving someone the right to buy the stock? Shouldn't you just buy the options?

Hold on to the question for a minute and let's look at the whole picture.

> *There is no Dummy here. It is a matter of investment strategy. Both of you had an ROI. There is one difference. Your profit (ROI) was <u>guaranteed</u> even though it was significantly lower percentage wise. After selling the Call, your portfolio is now worth $2088 ($2000 +100 -$12) a gain of $88 in two months—that's <u>2.18% a month</u>.*

Now look. In our example everything went in the right direction. But that isn't always the case as we know. Remember, there are three things that can happen:

1. *The stock increases in value which is the case we chose*
2. *The stock remains the same with no loss or gain and finally*
3. *The stock loses value.*

If in fact 1 and 2 are the case you still keep the $200 that you were paid for the option and you still own the stock. Cuz is ok with 1 but with 2 or 3 Cuz loses everything.

So two out of three times you win and two out of three times the call buyer loses.

If the stock is equal to or less than $20 at expiration, the option is worthless. Cuz loses his money.

It is yours. Go buy lollipops for the kids—or for yourself for that matter.

No wait!

Don't forget your strategy here. You are going to reinvest. You are going to reinvest the entire $2088 and do this for lots of years.

Raise your right hand and swear!

So the answer to the question is pretty obvious—

"You sold him the call so you can be guaranteed an income of $88 in two months".

Keep in mind the essence of what you are doing. You are looking for a monthly income that is pretty sure to happen with little risk.

EXERISE!

Go to Appendix B. Plug in the multiplier of 1.0218 which is a profit of 2.18 % per month and an initial capital of $2000. This will net you $346,322 in 20 years. And you are going to have a lot of fun doing it.

> *If you look at Sheet 2 in appendix B, with adding as little as $50 every two months you will net $741,186 in 20 years.*

Are you going to make 2.18% every month? This is entirely feasible. Your level of expertise will be up to you,

> **Now all this is based on selecting a stock and selling the call with the proviso that you compound your growth. In the next chapters we will develop the techniques you will want to boldly move forward!**
>
> **As Buzz would say "To infinity and beyond".**

Chapter 2

Picking the Right Stock

*C*hapter 1 gave a brief description and samples of real options. We talked about buying a stock and selling a call option—giving the right to someone else to buy the stock from us at a later date and at a predetermined price, or strike price.

You can also think of a covered call as a way of reducing the cost of a stock and at the same time generating income. If I buy a stock at $10 and I sell a right to buy the stock from me for fifty cents ($0.50) then the stock only cost me $9.50. I paid $10, got $.50 for each share when I sold the right to someone to buy the stock from me at the Strike Price. So my cost is actually $9.50. Now the buyer obviously thinks the stock is going up and more importantly it will go up more than $0.50 before the option expires otherwise he loses his money.

Ok, so how do we go about finding the right stock to rent! Let's look at the basics once more. We want to invest enough in the stock so that we would like to get at least one hundred shares to sell one contract.

Without having at least 100 shares of the stock, we cannot sell a call contract. That gives us a narrow range for the stock price initially. If the price was $10 a share we could effectively purchase 200 shares and sell (write) two contracts. In the present makeup of online brokers the commission for buying 100 shares of a stock or 2000 shares is the same. Let' assume the stock is priced at $10. If we purchase 200 shares it will cost us $2000 plus a commission which would be on the order of $12 depending upon the Broker. So we need to cough up $2012 for our purchase.

Lay a guilt trip on Granny and get the bucks already!

These low commissions are the one big advantage of the online trading that is prevalent today. If we hired a full time broker we would need a few hundred bucks plus to do a simple transaction. Most brokers are not worth the additional cost. We will be our own broker and control our own destiny. Keep the profit for yourself!!

Step 1 Select a stock by price and call option

Knowing that you have limited funds in the beginning, it is necessary to find a stock that is reasonable in price and **optionable.**

Ok. Time to talk about optionable stocks. Not every stock on the market is optionable. That is you cannot buy or sell the options on the stock because they are non existent! The Options Market sets the pace for whether or not a particular equity can be optioned. There are several rules that govern the optionability of a stock and is a very complex subject and not intended to be thoroughly discussed here. Options have their own Exchange—The Chicago Board of Options Exchange (CBOE).

Our concern is with the value of the option, not how it was established. It is valuable to understand the variables that play in the computation of an option, but only to the extent it makes you aware that options are fragile indicators of the stocks movement. The Black-Scholes formula was developed to determine the true price of a stock using certain variables.

It is not the intent of this book to make the reader an expert in option handling. The intent is to aid in the development of a skill in using the Call option to generate income on a repetitive basis in conjunction with purchasing a stock. We will concentrate on the right combination of stock and call option that will allow us to generate a monthly income which can be reinvested and compounded to accrue a goodly sum.

Getting back to our mission. We are looking for the best return for our money in terms of percentage for compounding and subsequent growth.

To be consistent, we will set our minimum target at $3.5% per month and pick our stock accordingly.

*Suppose you select an optionable stock whose price is $20 and a **two month** option is selling for fifty cents ($.50).*

If all you have is $2000 then you know immediately that all you can buy is 100 shares and sell one call (100 shares) *at $0.50 a share. That means that you net $50 for the sale. (100 shares x $.50)*

So right off the bat you recognize that this is only 2.5% (($50/$2000) x 100%) for two months or 1.25% per month.

Let's do the math anyway.

Price	Cost (100 shares)	Option Sale	ROI (2mos)	
$20	$2000	$.50	$50	2.5%
			$50/$2000 x100%	

*This means that we netted approximately **1.25%** per month.*

We have to get at least 7% for a two month option since we are looking for an average of 3.5% per month.

We are really short of our target of 3.5% per month so we pass on this one!

In order for this stock to be in our portfolio we want the call option to net us $140 (.07 x $2000) for two months. That means the call has to sell for $1.40 per share.

If I tell you how much a stock will cost it is easy to determine the value of a call necessary to achieve 3.5% per month. Take the total cost and multiply it by the number of months times 3.5%. For a two months option you need 7% and for a three month option you need 10.5%. Let's take a look!

Total Cost x (Nr. Of Months x 3.5%) = Necessary income

Table 1

Cost of Stock	2 Mos.7% Income	Sell 100 Shares Price per share	3 Mos. (10.5%) Income	Sell 100 Shares Price per share
$1000	$70	$0.70	$105	$1.05
$1500	$105	$1.05	$157.50	$1.60
$2000	$140	$1.40	$210	$2.10

If the purchase price of the stock is $1000 then you must make $70 (7%) on the sale for a two month call and $105 (10.5%) for a three month call.

Let' say we see a nice $15 stock and the two month options are $1.10 ea. Looking at the above I know I am above the required $1.05. I can buy 100 shares for $1500 and sell 1 contract for $110. This gives me an income of 7.3% ($110/$1500=7.33%) for two months. BINGO!

I could make a chart in Excel that would cover every possibility that you could encounter even when you are spending well over one hundred thousand dollars.

So I did. It is included in Appendix A.

It is called CHART 3.5%.

Say thank you!!

If you find an interesting stock, just plug in the stock price, the call option price and the option expiration period and it will tell you what monthly percentage you will get and how much it will cost. This can be done for one or several contracts. You guessed it. If you change the percentage field, this chart will work for any percentage that you desire. When you get better at this you might want to shoot for 5% or so. NICE!

*After awhile you won't need this **CHART 3.5%.** It is convenient in the beginning. All you need are the basics. For a 2 month option we need 7% and for a 3 month we need 10.5% to get 3.5% per month!*

I know this is getting repetitious but we want this to be second nature to you so that you can glance at a stock and tell if it meets the basic criteria. Once we select a stock based on the expected income we now look at some of the basics that make the stock a good choice.

Step 2 Evaluate The Fundamentals

There are three fundamental properties that we will look at. These are easily viewed in your online account information. All online accounts have an analysis section that will display the fundamental properties of just about all market stocks.

If you are a Market Buff there are certain properties of a stock that you will undoubtedly be familiar with, such as Price Earnings Ratio, Market Cap, Volatility and a host of other parameters that will give you a sense of the value of the stock. But I am going to give you what I consider to be the most valuable properties that you should consider when you choose a stock for Covered Call Writing.

These properties are:

News

Market Expert Consensus

Trend-line

I consider these the fundamentals.

*In the chapter on Market Strategies we will develop the reasons why these properties are important. Suffice it to say that we are not trying to learn the Market in general but we are sincerely trying to learn one simple strategy—***Covered Call Writing!***

Our desire is to get called out—lose the stock—so that we are only keeping a stock for two or three months—that's it!!

In the Covered Call Writing process, we don't care if the option is executed or it expires. If it expires then the stock did not move or it moved in the wrong direction. This is normal for many stocks. What it means to you is only significant if the movement downward is extreme. If it stays the same at expiration or it drops slightly you just turn right around and resell another option.

If on the other hand, the stock tanks or drops, say more than 10% of its value, then caution and patience are necessary. Does this happen. You bet it does! There are several strategies to employ depending on why the stock dropped so strongly and the present strength indicators. Refer to Chapter 5—Market Strategies.

Stay the course with this material and you will really get good at this!!

Chapter 3

Actual Trades

*L*et's look at <u>actual trades</u> to illustrate the point of keeping our goals in mind when we are selecting a particular stock. We are going to start with a reasonable Granny account of $2000, so our price range should be between $5 and $15. The following transactions used stocks that fell into the required beginning price range. Later examples will illustrate higher priced stocks with much larger investments.

These stocks were selected using a list of stocks by price and an indicator that the stock has associated options. The stocks traded in these examples were selected from a charting system which had the capability to filter stocks by price, options, market sectors and a host of other parameters which made it very convenient for Covered Call Writing.

Without a convenient list of this nature, this could be a tedious task. When you look for stocks with your online broker service you must know how to search for the details.

All the necessary information is there but it is not as accessible as other systems. **We talk more about Charting systems in Chapter 4.**

Recall that there are two basic steps to Writing a Covered Call. We are going to refer to these steps as Leg 1 and Leg 2.

Leg 1: We purchase the stock and sell the call.

Leg 2: We track the progress of the stock and take action if required.

Take a look at the following actual transaction for Cirrus Logic Inc

(Symbol-CRUS). This transaction took place in the first quarter of 2007.

Leg 1

The following table shows Leg 1 of an actual Covered Call transaction that occurred in January of 2007.

Date	Sym.	Price	Qty.	Cost of Stock	Opt. Strk. & Exp.	Opt. Sold	Opt. Price	$ Rcvd	Give Back	Expected Profit
1/16/07	crus	$7.89	200	$1579	..					
1/16/07					$7.5 Feb	200	$0.70	$140	$78	$62

Take a close look at the option price and the stock price. Remember, we would like to see a minimum of 3.5% return per month. A fast calculation shows that the option price of $0.70 is almost 10% of the stock price which is $7.89. This *is a fairly good indicator that this was a promising Covered Call situation and notice that the option is for one month only. At 3.5% of the stock price we would require an option price of only twenty eight cents ($0.28). The option price is more than double this. (You can use the Chart 3.5% calculator in Appendix A for a one month option).*

But Wait, you say, there is another variable that is introduced here. You did say that-right?

What is this Give Back column?

Ok! This is the real world of stock prices. In our chapter 2 example we used numbers that were conveniently selected for the purpose of clarity. <u>Remember we said that option strike prices were usually issued at intervals of $2.50</u>. In the real world, the price of the stock does not normally equal the option strike price. Another way of saying this is that it is not "At the Money". You will see this as you go.

If the price of the stock is greater than the Strike price (the price you are selling it for) then the difference is the Give Back—or the "In the Money" Amount. In this case we sold the $7.50 Call which is lower than the value of the stock. Therefore we are losing (Giving Back) the difference between the strike and the stock value ($0.39 a share x 200 shares) or $78.

Leg 2

The second leg entails tracking the progress of the stock and taking any required action. This stock sold for over $7.50 a share at expiration. Since it was called away at the strike we assume it was higher than $7.50 per share. Normally, as will *be shown in future examples, we will know the price of the stock at option expiration. We no longer own the stock.*

Total Cost for 200	Stock Called Away	Income from sale of stock	Income From Options	Total Income	Profit= Total Income Minus Total Cost	ROI
$1579	Yes	$1500	$140	$1640	$61	3.9%
		(200x7.5)	(200x0.7)		$1640-$1579	

This stock earned us 3.9% in one month and the stock was called away.

Analysis:

The Return On Investment was 3.9%. This means that I had $61 more than we had one month prior.

I bought 200 shares of the stock for $1575 and sold the February Call for $0.70 each. Note that this was a one month call—that is, it expired in a month. So I sold the right to someone to buy the stock at the strike price of $7.50 but he had only one month in which the option could be exercised.

The stock cost $7.89 a share but I was willing to sell the stock to someone for $7.5??. You bet! The price was right—$140.

What was the Call Buyer's exposure?

He paid me $140. Let's assume that he exercised the option immediately and turned around and sold the stock on the market. He bought it for $7.50 a share and sold it for $7.89 a *share. He paid $1500 ($7.50 x 200) for the stock and would have sold it for $1578 (200 x $7.89).*

So the purchase of the option had an immediate value of $78 or was In the Money by $78.

Obviously it would have made <u>no sense</u> for the buyer to do this. He collected $78 but his cost would have been $140 to buy the option. The only reason that he would have paid you $140 is because he thought this stock was going up. <u>Essentially he was gambling that the stock would increase more than $0.70 per share, which is what he paid you for the option.</u>

He was betting that the stock would be at or above $8.20 per share before the option expired. Since the stock was already at $7.89 a share, all he needed to get his investment back was $0.31 per share. If he exercised the option and sold the stock at $8.20 he would have netted $0.70 per share (or $140) which is exactly what he paid for it. <u>This is called the break-even point for the buyer.</u>

So the buyer hoped (gambled!) that the stock would move up more than $0.31 per share so he could make some quick cash. In this case, we do not have the final price so we do not know how "right" the buyer was.

By way of illustration, let's assume the stock was $8.70 per share at option expiration. The buyer made $0.50 per share or $100 (200 x $.50). Let's look.

Bought the 200 shares for $1500 (200 x $7.50)

Sold the stock for $8.70 or (200 x $8.70) = $1740
He would have received $1740-$1500=$240
Subtracting his cost of the option -$140
He Nets $100 or $0.50 Per share.

In this assumption, the Buyer's ROI could have been ($100/$140) or 71.5%, which is pretty nice!

Just to annoy you, let's do a recap on everything.

Naw! Just Kidding—You got it

Here is another transaction with a slightly different chart:

Covered 2009 for SBH

Date								
19-Oct	Stock	Price	Shares	Comm.	Cost			
	SBH	$7.65	200	9.99	1539.99			
21-Nov	Option	Opt. Price	Income from Option Sale	Comm.		Fees	Realized Income	
	Nov 7.5	$0.6	$120	$13.74		0.03	$106.23	**ROI=6.89%**
								=(106.23/ 1539.99)

The price of this stock at option expiration was $7.49 and was not assigned to the call owner—I maintained ownership of the stock.

In this case I used a little more detail and included all the commissions and fees. I do this from time to time as an exercise to assess the total impact. You should develop Excel programs to keep track of progress.

Notice a few things here:

1. *This is a one month option and realized a 6.89% ROI. Very Nice!*
2. *This call is in the money by $0.15—Price $7.65—Strike $7.5*
3. *There is no mention of the Give Back of $0.15. It is not always necessary to list the give back separately since it is factored in the transaction cost. I like to include it at times just for clarity.*

Here are a few more actual transactions. These were done with larger sums upfront.

	Symbol	Exp.	Bought	Sold	Price	Total Cost	Option Sale	Called	Total Income	Profit	%	
Stock	CYD		3000		$7.60	$22,631						
Option	GMQCU	Mar. 7.5		9	$0.35		$298		$298	$797	3.5%	
				21	$0.25		$499		$499			
Stock	CYD		3000					$22,470				
Option	CYDDU	Apr. 7.5		30	$0.80		$2,367		$2,367	$2,207	9.8%	Assigned
Stock	HL		3000		$7.60	$22,811		$22,479				
Option	HLCU	Mar. 7.5		30	$0.35		$1,017		$23,497	$686	3.0%	Assigned
Stock	RZ		3200		$5.00	$16,010		$15,970				
Option	RZDA	Apr. 5		31	$0.30		$897		$16,867	$857	5.4%	Assigned
Stock	AOB		2000		$10.58	$21,170		$19,970				
Option	AOBEB	10-May		20	$0.85		$1,675		$21,645	$475	2.2%	Assigned

There are significant points of interest in these trades. Notice the first trade.

I Bought 3000 shares of CYD for $22,631 and sold the March $7.50 Call Options in <u>two batches</u> for a total income of $797 ($298 + $499).

When you attempt to sell a call at a certain strike it is never a given that you can. This will depend on a number of issues such as the Open Interest in the option and the direction in which the stock is trending at the time you want to sell.

The bid/ask spread on options can change radically from hour to hour. Notice that one batch of 9 contracts (900 shares) was sold at $0.35 and the remainder of 21 contracts was sold at $0.25. I obviously lowered my sell price after evaluating the situation with regards to the market conditions, the number of bidders, potential ROI and just the right timing. Since there were not enough buyers for the option at $0.35 I waited for the next best opportunity after considering the interest in the options and the remaining time to expiration. This is something you will get a "feel" for as you go!

At the March expiration date, the stock was lower than the Strike price by an amount sufficient to deter any of the option buyers from exercising their right to buy the stock at $7.50. The options expired, and I retained the stock. At a cost of $22,631 and a profit of $797, I had an ROI of 3.5%.

Now I turned right around and sold 30 contracts of the April $7.50 call for $0.80 each with an income of $2,367.

Take notice of the call value of $0.80. Remember we said that if the option makers thought that the stock was trending up, the sell price of the option would reflect this. This was the case and the option was selling for over twice as much as the $0.35 for the March options.

In April the stock was called away from me and I received $22,470 for the sale of 3000 shares at the strike price of $7.50 per share. The commission cost for the sale of the stock was $30.

The original cost of the stock was $22,631 and the profit from the sale of the calls was $2,367 yielding a Return On Investment of 9.8%. This is a one month ROI.

Here is a strong case for the Covered Call strategy. I actually made a ROI of 3.5% + 9.8% for a total of 13.3%. Notice that there is no purchase date for the first transaction with the March calls, so I cannot arrive at an accurate Monthly ROI. I rarely go for an option that is longer than two months. I purchased the stock in February and sold the calls two months prior to April then the average Monthly ROI is 1.75% for the first two months (March-April) and the monthly ROI for May was 9.8%.

Now, let's move on to Opening an Online Account!

Chapter 4

Opening an Online Account

*G*et *your Granny Bucks ready because it is time to start the fun. The first step is to make sure that you have a good computer setup. Get your Geek friend to give you all the latest requirements as to speed, capabilities etc. As a minimum you will require Microsoft Excel.*

The next step is to do some search homework and look at all the available Online Trading companies. I use Ameritrade, Scottrade and E-Trade. There are subtle differences in each but the essentials are all there in each one. Each one has different capabilities with respect to stock analysis, display, money transfer capabilities and a host of other items. You will find discussions on risk analysis, futures trading, options trading, banking etc. etc.

When you decide on the one you want to start with, get familiar with the commission structure and the basic procedures for buying and selling stocks and options.

There will be forms to fill out, but I want you to talk to someone at the company. The best thing you can do is to tell your contact what you intend to do. "I am going to be an expert at Covered Calls". Sounds good to any one. Now you will get someone who isn't really interested in you in particular but he will be interested in getting you to the right seminars or knowledge pages that will lead you in the right direction.

Tell anyone you can talk to how you want to open your account. You will need the following three capabilities as a minimum.

Options Trading
Stock Trading
Electronic Funds Transfer

Depending upon the type of account and how the account is funded, it will probably take about a week to get the account ready to trade. Decline all special services that come with a price tag—at least initially. You want to get a lot of experience with the account before you do anything other than the basic maneuvers for Covered Calls. Do not be shy about asking questions. Seek all the help you can get on the site, especially with respect to Covered Call Writing. Remember, you are the one who is footing the bill here and you want to make money for yourself and Granny too!

Buy-Write

To make matters a little easier for the investor, many Brokers have programs that will enable you to complete the first Leg of the covered call writing procedure with one action. This is called a Buy-Write procedure. Remember there are two Legs to covered call writing. Buy-Write is a term that is used to accomplish the Leg 1 tasks for a Covered Call in one fell swoop. Leg 1 is buying the stock and selling the call. Doing a Buy—Write allows you to accomplish both tasks at the same time. Make sure you discuss a Buy-Write with your contact and understand the commissions.

I personally do not use the Buy Write capabilities because it requires a little work on the part of the broker and I have found that Online Accounts have the very basic problem which I call "lack of human intervention".

As you become more familiar with the terms and feel more comfortable with the basic procedures for Covered Call Writing you will realize that a Buy-Write tool could be extremely useful and should be thoroughly investigated with your Online Broker. All three of the above mentioned Brokers have tutorials and seminars and educational articles on Buy Writes and almost any other subject that you will need in order to be an efficient trader. They are extremely helpful. Just get used to doing the work yourself.

The tools most On-Line Brokers offer will serve you well to find a stock symbol and associated ask price, the appropriate call to sell and the bid /ask of the call. The calculation of potential return is generally available but they may or may not include commissions. Remember selecting a stock with a high priced call is the crux of the effort and Broker supplied tools could save you a LOT of time.

There is a CAUTION here! In order to do a selection of a stock with a high priced call it is necessary to use volatility *as a search criteria, since highly volatile stocks usually have a higher call price. Any program offered by the Broker will most certainly be looking for the highest selling price for a call which means a high volitility. We will talk a little more about this in the next section when we get to the criteria for selecting stocks, but high volatility in a stock is not a good feature for covered call writing. **We are looking for little or no movement in the stock price for the option period.***

When you perform a Buy Write action you will request a Net transaction. Essentially it entails specifying the Net result of buying a stock and selling a call at the same time. There is no exotic anything here.

If for example, the stock is $10 and the call that you want to sell is $1 then the Net cost to you is $9. You buy 100 shares of the stock for $1000 and sell One Call (100 shares) for $100 ($1 x 100 shares) so your Net Cost is $900 or $9 a share. This is called a Net Debit since your account will be debited $900.

*These systems often consider more variables than I like. Our strategy is to be concerned with strike prices that are At-the-Money or close. The idea is to make very small but consistent gains without worrying about a large movement in stock price. (**At the Money is when the stock price and the strike price are the same.**)*

It is not the intention here to delve into the various programs that are available with present day Brokers. The point is that these Broker supplied tools are very helpful if you continue to do your homework and investigate the proper parameters of the chosen stock. These systems are meant as a customer service only with disclaimers.

There will be several terms that you will become familiar with in the course of your transactions. Two terms are worth discussing here.

Market Price
Limit Price

A transaction that is done at the Market price is implemented almost immediately. If you are buying a stock at Market you are willing to pay the price that the seller is asking for (Ask Price)—so it is a fast deal. Additionally, if you sell a call at the market it is immediately executed because you are willing to sell the call at the price that someone is willing to pay (Bid Price).

This is not normally a profitable situation in that the Bid and Ask prices are always the prices that someone is trying to get a bargain with. If you buy and sell at Market you are at the mercy of the **Market Maker.** He is not obligated to give you a specific price if you trade at the Market. Usually the price is very close to the asking price if you are buying, but it can be radically different.

Let us assume that two different people want to sell the same stock at different prices. Customer A wants $10 but customer B only wants $9.80. The market maker receives both requests and in the Bid Ask spread he uses the lower asking price to entice buyers into the arena. If you come along and buy at the Market, he can legitimately sell you the higher price of $10 because theoretically he can make the case that the price can change at any given moment.

*The same holds true for sale of the call. If you sell it at Market he can legitimately sell the call at a lower price. Obviously this is unacceptable since you are trying to attain a certain profit level (ROI) you must be able to control the selection of prices. **Never buy or sell anything at Market**.*

Limit Price

*The answer to this dilemma is a **Limit Transaction** by which the Market Maker is obligated to give you the price you ask for or a more favorable one. If for example you are asking to sell a call at a limit price of **X** he cannot sell the call at a lower price than **X** but he can sell at a higher price which of course is more favorable to you. The same holds true for a limit purchase of a stock at **Y** price. He can not sell you the stock at any price higher than **Y** but he can sell you the stock at a lower price which is more favorable to you.*

The use of the system with practice is simple and straightforward. When you buy the stock you will be asked to input the stock symbol, the number of shares, the time period that you want etc. etc.

Let' look at an example.

A Stock Order

*When you are in your account and you want to place an order to buy or sell **a stock** you will be presented with a table something like this.*

Your Name	Account #	Your Purchasing Power Or funds Available			
Order Type?	Quantity?	Symbol?	BID Size	ASK Size	Volume
Price Type	Limit Price	Term			

The format for this input form will be different for just about all Online Systems, but the basic information is the same.

Most start with some information about you and your account. Your name and account number will appear automatically. Some of the information is for convenience such as the "Purchasing Power or Funds Available"— presented to remind you of what you can buy.

You will be asked to input several items such as order type, stock symbol, quantity and type of price you want to obtain. These will usually be in the form of a drop-down table from which you will select what you want.

The quantity is straightforward and is simply the number of shares that you wish to purchase.

The stock symbol fill-in simply asks you to enter the symbol or if you know the stock name you can select here to pull up the symbol.

Price type has a number of selections which will vary with the Broker such as—. Market, Trailing Stop, Limit etc. You *will want Limit. When you become proficient at the trading business you can dabble into other price selections and other strategies, if you wish.*

Once you specify Limit you now have to indicate the price you want to pay for this stock. The Bid/Ask spread will appear immediately.

The last box asks for the time for which you want this bid to be valid. Various options will appear here including "good for the day". If you select "good for the day" and you do not get the call purchased before the market closes on that day, your order will be canceled. If the stock is not purchased you can always re-enter your order the next day.

This order procedure varies somewhat with all On-Line brokers.

This example is merely intended to give you a feel for the type of inputs needed to buy your stock. You will get totally familiar with the various procedures as you go.

Notice that there is an additional click on the bottom that allows you to preview the order. Always preview your order to prevent errors.

Option Order

An option order entry is the same with slightly different inputs required.

The Order Type
    Either Sell or Buy. With covered Calls this is always Sell.

Contracts

Number of contracts you want to sell. Remember that one contract equals 100 shares. If, as an example you want to sell options on 300 shares, then you would input 3.

Type

This asks whether you are talking about a Call or a Put. In our case this is a Call.

Expiration

Enter here the Month in which the option expires. Once you enter this info a Bid/Ask spread should appear automatically.

Strike Price

Enter the Strike Price of the option.

A Buy-Write form will require other inputs such as Net Debit etc. You should get a full explanation from your Broker as to the procedures for filling out all order entry forms. Usually the On-line broker will have a Knowledge or Information section with all the required instructions.

CHARTING SYSTEMS

Ultimately you will want a good charting system to refer to.

Charting systems are God's gift to Covered Call Writers. It used to be that the good charting systems were very expensive and often complex to learn. What the Covered Call expert is looking for in a charting system can be obtained with some of the most popular systems on the market today. One thing you should have is a ready list of stocks that are:

1. *Optionable*
2. *Within a certain Price Range*
3. *Trend lines*
4. *Have Associated News*
5. *Bid/Ask Details*

It is invaluable for a Covered Call Writer to have a list of every stock on the Market at his fingertips. Just the ability to separate stocks that fit certain criteria that you like is a big plus. Most charting systems are able to select stocks based on individual parameters that you yourself specify.

Here you have to do your homework. I advise that you start slowly. Use the information available with a free charting system to get the feel of what you are doing. Yes, there are some that are free, or at least low priced and easily affordable. The first thing you must do is to discuss this issue with your Online Broker. Do not hesitate to tell them that you do not want to pay for the service, at least initially. They will recommend the ones that they think are appropriate.

As you get more and more sophisticated you will search out the best systems.

I personally used the Worden Brothers Telechart system. As charting systems go, this system tends toward the expensive side but it is well worth the price. The ability to create your own portfolio of criteria driven lists is a powerful tool. You can create a list of stocks based on the parameters that you choose. As an example you can select stocks that are within a certain price range, are optionable and are trending upward. Good stuff.

Again, go online, search for stock charting systems and do your homework!!!

Chapter 5

Market Strategies—Making Your Money Grow

*O*kay it is time to talk Turkey about the downside of any equity investment. Talk Turkey is "Old Guy Speak" for what are the facts. You knew of course that you would someday face a downside. That's when the stock price takes a dip or dive in value. Well, let's look at some strategies that we can employ to help us recover any losses while writing covered calls.

Look, it is fairly obvious by now that we have a reasonably good strategy in that there are two out of three situations for the covered call that will make us money. These are when the call is In the Money or At the Money at expiration. When we have a potential loss is when the call is out of the Money at option expiration.

So let's first review the various scenarios that can take place when dealing with Covered Calls.

#1 *At Option expiration, the stock price is higher.*

We know that our objective is met in a covered call when the price of the stock you are renting is higher at option expiration. *This is the ideal situation.* Everyone makes money. You get to keep the profits from the sale of the Call Option and the Option purchaser sells the option for a profit. Simply stated, the stock gets called away and we keep the money for the sale of the call. There are no strategies here that will improve the immediate situation.

Let's do the numbers for a situation where the stock moves up. We are going to use more realistic numbers where the purchase price does not coincide with a strike price as set by the options market. Remember, contract strikes are usually every $2.50 (i.e. $10—$12.50—$15 etc.) so that a stock that is selling for $11.50 is not at any particular strike price. You can either sell the $12.50 strike or the $10 strike depending on which is the most favorable and least risk.

Some stocks in the present day market also have $1 increments for strike prices. This will depend on the stock and you will become more familiar with this as you go.

Note: We can sell a call with a strike price above or below the purchase price. This will be decided by which is more advantageous!

For our example we will choose to write a call that is below the Market price because the call price is attractive.

We look at XYZ corp. which is now priced at $11.50. It has good credentials and the $10 option is attractive. So we buy

100 shares of XYZ. This is a typical Covered Call operation. In this example we are starting with an investment of only $850 and ending with $1000 two months later. This averages out to earnings of over 8% a month.

Here Goes!!

Cost of Stock	$1,150	(100 shares)
Sell 1 Call Contract for	$3.00 /Share	
Take in	$300	
Actual Cost of Stock	$850	($1150-$300)
Call Contract Expiration	2 Mos.	
Call Contract Strike	$10	
At Option Expiration	+ $1000 Sell 100 shares at $10 ea.	
	+ $300 Sale of Calls	
	- $1150 Cost of Stock	
Profit	$150	

Another way of looking at the profit of this transaction is by taking the actual money gotten for the sale of the 100 shares at strike price ($10 each) or $1000 and subtracting the actual cost of the stock of $850 ($1150-$300) =$150. So you invest $850 and get back $1000.

ROI	17.6%	($150/$850) x 100%

The following chart (Chart 1) represents a movement in purchased stock. The stock moves up in value over the option validity period of 60 Days.

Chart 1

Day	Stock Price	Option Ask Price	Days Rem.
1	$11.50	$3.00	60
15	$11.80	$3.30	45
25	$12.30	$3.80	35
30	$12.40	$3.90	30
40	$12.20	$3.00	20
50	$12.10	$2.30	10
Exp.	$12.10	$2.30	0

<u>A call option has two values; Intrinsic and Time. The call sells for $3—Intrinsic value is $1.50 (it is above the strike price by $1.50) and the Time value is $1.50 for the 2 Months remaining until expiration.</u>

Allrighty Then! Here is what we have!

Day 1 shows the basic status of the stock when purchased. Notice the Option was sold for $3. This is a $10 strike price option which means that the call is in the money by $1.50—the intrinsic value.

The Option Buyer is obviously anticipating that within the next 60 days the stock will go over $13.00 which is his break even point where he neither gains nor loses money—the price at which the option is worth $3.00 as a minimum.

Day 15 shows the stock moving upward in price. The stock has gained $0.30. The Option Buyer is now anticipating the stock reaching the "above $13 Price" so he is now looking to sell the option at a higher price of $3.30. He has time on his side since there are still 45 days left to expiration.

Day 25 shows the stock moving even higher and there are still 35 days remaining before option expiration. The stock has increased by another $0.50 or a total of $0.80. So the Option Buyer is asking $3.80. This will give him a profit of $0.80 per share.

Day 30 also shows a small movement upwards so up goes the asking price to $3.90.

Day 40 now shows the stock pulling back to $12.20 with only 20 days left to option expiration. The Time Value is running out. The Intrinsic value is only $2.20. At this point the Option Buyer may want to break even in light of the fact that the stock looks like it is not moving rapidly enough to make $13 in only 20 days. He now tries to get his initial investment back so he is willing to sell his option for $3.00.

Day 50 shows that the stock is flattening at $12.10 with only 10 days to expiration. The chances of this stock getting to or above the target of $13 are getting very slim indeed. The Option Buyer now wants to settle for what he can get. He drops his price to $2.30.

This option is running out of time. If the Option Buyer thinks the stock is going much lower he might drop his asking price to say $2.00 which is $0.10 lower than the intrinsic value. This will almost guarantee that the options maker or someone will *buy the option and make a fast $0.10 per share. The purpose here is to stop his loss at $1. (Paid $3 and sells for $2)*

Get the feel of this. All of the burden here is with the Option Buyer. Time, when it gets short is an option owner's enemy. You on the other hand, as the Covered Call Writer (option seller) will reach your goal even if the stock ends up at $11.50. *Even if the stock goes lower than $11.50 you might still see a small profit.*

Realize that the call owner can just wait until the option expires and he will be assigned the stock at $10 a share. He then turns around and sells it on the Market. In this case it means that the stock is higher than $10 a share at option expiration. Using our example of $12.10—the Market value at expiration—he makes $2.10 on each share but he paid $3. He has a net loss of $0.90 a share or $90.

You, the covered call writer still have a gain of $150 or 17.6%.

This stock is going to be called away from you—assigned to the Option Buyer—because the option is in the money even though the Option Buyer will lose money.

This is a scenario that plays out very frequently in the options market. A great majority of options expire worthless or with reduced value.

> ***But you are the Covered Call Writer and you end up with the $150 gain.***

Oh! Happiness and bliss. Buy some cigars!

Remember, we are looking at the situation where the stock goes up in value. IF IF IF the stock had gone to say $14—both you and the option owner would have made money. You would have made the same $150 and he would have made $100. His break even price was $13 so he sells the stock for a gain of a buck a share.

IF IF IF the stock had gone to $18 the call option owner would have made $5 a share or $500 and guess what you would have made—that's right—$150.

IF IF IF the stock had gone up to $30 the option owner would have made $17 a share or $1700 and you would have made that same $150.

I think you get the point. When you do a covered call you limit your upside gain potential. But remember why you are doing this. It is to use a solid strategy that will almost guarantee your ROI.

There will be plenty of times when you will look at the gain that the stock makes and wish you had never sold the call and tied up the stock. These are the times when you have to be committed to your end result of slow and steady gains to achieve your goal of accrued cash.

#2 <u>*At option expiration, the stock price is equal to or lower than the strike price.*</u>

What happens when the stock flattens or trends downward during the option period. We have two things to consider—is the stock value equal to or lower than the Strike price? First we will handle the equality issue.

#2A. Stock Price=Strike Price at Expiration

We are going to use the same stock example to illustrate what happens when the stock ends up at option expiration equal to the strike price.

Let's Look:

Again, XYZ is $11.50 when you bought it and you sell100 shares (one contract) of the $10 call for $3. That gets you $300 and it is a two month option.

You spend $1150 and take in $300 less an in the money amount of $1.50 x 100 shares or $150. You realize a $150 gain ($300-$150). During the two months the stock itself starts to drop in value. After the first month into the option period the stock drops to $10 a share. It stays at $10—the strike price now equals the stock price—for the next month and the option expires.

Here We Go Again

Cost of Stock	$1,150	
Sell 1 Call Contract for	$3.00 /Share	
Take in	$300	
Actual Cost of Stock	$850	($1150-$300)
Call Contract Expiration	60 Days	
Call Contract Strike	$10	

Notice, we have a Break Even Point of $8.50 per share.

At option expiration (60 days after you sell the call) the stock dropped to a market value of $10 which is equal to the strike price.

Value of stock at market $1000   *(100 shares x $10 ea.)*

Net Gain   *$150*

Chart 2

Day	Stock Price	Days To Option Expiration	Market Value 100 Shares
1	$11.50	60	$1150
15	$11.80	45	$1180
25	$11.30	35	$1130
30	$11.00	30	$1100
40	$10.60	20	$1060
50	$10.30	10	$1030
Exp.	$10.00	0	$1000

What happened? Even though the stock pulled all the way back to the strike price (dropped $1.50 in value) you still made the same $150 on the transaction. Nice! You still own the stock but it has lost some value and it is now time to take a second look to see if the stock is worth keeping.

#2B The Stock Price is Less Than the Strike Price at Expiration.

Same scenario except that in this case the stock drops to $9, the option expires and you retain the stock at the lower price of $9. You now have a gain of $0.50 per share.

Let's look at the numbers. Remember, you still get the $150 for the call sale but your portfolio looks like this.

Cost of Stock	*$1,150*	
Sell 1 Call Contract for	*$3.00 /Share*	
Take in	*$300*	
Actual Cost of Stock	*$850*	*($1150-$300)*
Call Contract Expiration	*60 Days*	
Call Contract Strike	*$10*	

At option expiration (60 days after you sell the call) the stock dropped to a market value of $9

Value of stock at market	*$900 (100 shares x $9 ea.)*
Net Gain	*$50 ($900-$850)*

This is a case where the stock dropped below the strike price but you still had a small profit since it did not reach the break even point.

The Break Even Price here is a stock price of $8.50. If in fact the stock ended up at $8.50 per share at option expiration you would be at the break even point—that is you got back what you paid.

It is now time to decide whether to keep the stock or sell it. If it is still exhibiting good credentials then you might want to keep the stock and sell another call for the next best period that you can find. Generally speaking when the fundamentals of the stock are still solid the call price will normally remain fairly high (indicating faith that the stock will go up) and you can act as if you just purchased the stock and are writing a new call.

Generally, if the drop in stock price for the option period is more than 10%—in this case it is $1.50 or 13%—I recommend selling the stock.

This is a experience call and you will get better at this as you go. My experience has been that if it is difficult to tell what made the price drop it is always better to get out of the position, even if the drop is less than 10%. In this case the only thing you have lost is time!

Remember, there are a ton of stocks that can be used for our purpose.

Recommendation: **Sell the stock if the drop is >10%**

                        Keep the stock if the drop is <10% only if the fundamentals are sound

The procedure here is to take a look at the stock fundamentals and also at the call prices.

#3. <u>At option expiration, the stock price is lower than the Break Even Price.</u>

In this case the stock ends up lower than the break even price of $8.50 per share This is a situation in which you have an unrealized loss. It is unrealized because you have not yet sold the stock.

Let's take a look.

The same XYZ stock which you purchased for $11.50 ends up significantly lower than the $10 strike price that you sold it for. Let us say that the stock, at option expiration has a market value of $8, which is $2 lower than the strike price. The percentage change in stock value is about 30%. ($3.5/$11.5). If you sell the stock you will have a realized loss of $200 for the transaction and if you keep the stock you will have an unrealized loss of $200.

Let's look.

Value of stock at Market	*+$800 (100 x $8)*	
Cost of the stock	*-$1150*	*(100 x $11.50)*
Loss due to stock value	*-$350*	
Income from Sale of Call	*+$300*	
Net Loss	*($50)*	

Recommendation: Take the Loss—Sell the Stock!!

*Ok, it is apparent that **Cases #1,#2A &B are acceptable** in that no loss is incurred. Case #1 is the ideal covered call and Case #2 can be either a break even transaction or a smaller than expected profit. Case #3 is an unrealized loss. If we sell the stock it is a realized loss.*

The question is can anything be done before the option expiration date that might reduce our loss or exposure to loss. It is your sworn duty to yourself to watch the progress of the stock periodically as the expiration day for the call option nears. Raise your left hand! (Your right hand is already up—I didn't tell you to lower it). Stay with the program.

So we buy the stock, monitor the progress periodically and apply strategies as we see fit.

In the back of your mind you can hear Granny scream!

What strategies? Where the Hell are the strategies?

She sees the stock going South of the Border and doesn't speak Mexican.

Hold on! Relax. We have a few tricks up our Serrape.

Take Granny out and explain that you are a genius.

Let's consider the three cases. Cases #1 and #2 do not need any special attention here except that in #2B we do a two minute review of the stocks fundamentals. Remember, it is not necessary to become an expert in any stock to be effective in covered call writing. I told you it was Good.

Fundamentals

So what are the fundamentals that we look at? In chapter 2 we briefly outlined what I consider the basic fundamentals—News, Market Expert Consensus and Trend-line.

1. *News*

There are a number of occurrences that will affect individual stocks or the entire Market. Look for News on the health of the stock and form your opinion as to good or bad. Here are some examples of items that affect the health of a stock. Anything that happens in the world might affect the Market in general. Threats of War, Economic Crisis Oversees, Living Conditions Etc. It is imperative that you keep abreast of the US and World news. Here we mention a few items that might affect the performance of a particular stock.

Job Layoffs.

The public generally looks upon Job Layoffs as a good move for the stock since work force reduction is initially followed by reduced expenses which prompts greater profitability. This is probably true for the short term but in all too many cases spells bad news in the long term.

Management Change

One of the most significant items that will turn a stock on its head or propel it to stardom is that of changing company officers—CEO, CFO or General Manager. This is perceived by the public to indicate a problem within the ranks or company structure. In most cases it is done to enhance the company's capabilities by bringing in a known expert or a more experienced person. In some instances, to cut the company's perceived bad reputation or to get rid of a" thought to be incompetent" person. Whatever the case is, changing the management structure has a negative impact—at least initially.

Downgrades

Another bad sign to the general public is a Sector downgrade. The Market is divided into sectors usually grouping same-same companies. Let's assume that Textiles is a leading market sector but a shortage of cotton, or silk is predicted. If your stock happens to be a clothing manufacturer or distributor, the public will view this as a downside and reflect their feelings by selling off stock that is perceived to be wholly dependent on these items.

Mergers and Takeovers

Mergers have a great impact on the health of a particular stock depending on how the Public perceives the Merger. Takeovers are by far the most volatile situation in the Market and almost always affect stock price.

2. *Market Experts Consensus*

Every Online Broker has a Cadre of experts that will form an opinion on the particular stock. Get to know these experts and especially pay attention to consensus experts. Consensus experts are groups of experts that form an average opinion of a particular stock. There might be as little four participants or as many as 12 in any consensus group.

Learn the track records of all the experts and make absolutely sure you understand the opinions of the experts. Remember, a stock that is not moving in either direction is a good candidate for Covered Call Writing. The two conditions that are the most favorable are a sideways moving stock or an up-trending stock.

Sideways moving stock might have a general consensus of "Hold". This might make it a good contender for Covered Call Writing. The major issue with a stock that is not moving is the price of the options. Usually if the Stock is stagnant the options are not selling for a good price.

A general consensus of "<u>Buy</u>" or "<u>Strong Buy</u>" is a great contender for a Covered Call. When a stock has a general consensus of "<u>Sell</u>" do not under any circumstances use this stock for covered call writing.

As an example, if you have 15 experts and 4 say sell, 4 say Buy and 7 say Strong Buy then you have a favorable skew—11 like the stock and 4 do not. Good choice for a Covered Call situation.

If the opposite is true and 11 do not like the stock and 4 do it is "no go".

3. <u>Trend-line</u>

There is an old market saying "The Trend is Your Friend".

This reverberates throughout the market even today. It basically says that you can base your evaluation of a stock by whether it is trending upward, staying flat or trending downward.

What we need to do here is to look at the stock's chart and determine the prevailing trend-line—that is, is it going up, down or is it flat.

There are two scenarios that work for the Covered Call and these are up or flat. A down trend is not a healthy thing.

There are reasons why stocks go down and these reasons must be respected.

Every Broker has a chart for almost every stock on the market. Once we learn how to read them effectively, we can easily determine the trend line.

There are a dozen or so more things that will affect the stock performance. When we look at the stock to see if it is still healthy for a Covered Call Situation we like to have all of these three fundamentals going the right way. If one of these is out of congruence with the others it is then time to sell the stock and move on to another

A. Strategies at Execution

When you buy a stock that you "feel" is going to move upward it is often prudent to wait a period of time before you sell the call option. If the stock moves up, the call option will be worth more and you may also have some value in writing a strike that is higher than the value of the stock. Also, if you have enough shares to enable you to split the sell process i.e. you have enough stock for at least two contracts (200 shares) then you may be able to enhance your profits. Here is an example.

Strategy 1   Sell Call Contracts Immediately

You purchase a stock for $11.10 and it looks like a strong uptrend is in progress. The $10 call is selling for $2.00. That is a $0.90 profit if you give up the stock at the $10 Strike.

You buy 200 shares (cost $2,220) with the intent to sell the calls for $2 with a two month contract. That is:

Cost of stock

200 x $11.10	-$2,220	
Sale of Calls	+$400	

Actual Cost — -$1820

Income (Called out of 200 shares at $10 a share.) — +$2,000

Profit (Income-Actual Cost) — +$180

ROI (2 Months) — 9.9% ($180/$1820)

You net $180 for the two month period i.e. (200 x $0.90) for a 4.9% monthly ROI.

Note:You are writing a call with a strike lower than the value of the stock which will almost guarantee that you will lose the stock.

Strategy 2   <u>Sell Contracts In Increments</u>

Strategy #1 was your original intent. But you really like this stock and it looks like a mover. Instead of selling both contracts for $2 each you sell only one contract and keep the other 100 shares open for a period. Remember, when you sell a contract, 100 shares of the stock are now locked up and unable to be used. By selling one contract you have locked in a small profit of $90. Now we wait about a week or two and see what happens.

Ok, you were right and the stock moves up $1 and is now worth $12.10. Now the options are going to be higher. But how much higher. If the time lapse is only two weeks out of the eight week option period then the loss in Time Value is small. There is an excellent chance that the option value will follow the stock increase on a one for one basis. That is the option will now sell for $3—an increase of $1.

Now is the time to sell the remaining contract for $300, which will now net you:

Value of stock 200 x $11.10			-$2,220
Sale of Calls	100 x $2	+$200	
	100 x $3	+$300	
			+$500
Actual Cost of stock			$1720
Income from sale of stock at Exp.			+$2,000
Profit Income-Cost		+$280	
ROI (2 Months)		15.3%	
		($280/$1820)	

Is this real? Yes. When you get experienced at this you will come across this situation. Now it does not look real impressive to increase your profits by another $100 or so, but **remember your mission—get the steady monthly ROI.**

Besides, there will be a time when you are buying 2000 shares as opposed to the 200 we are touting here and the increase of actual cash will be dynamic.

Strategy 3   <u>Wait for Better Strike Price</u>

This is yet another twist to strategy #2.

Let's suppose that we were able to get a good premium for the sale of the $12.5 strike. The stock value moved to $12.10 which is only $0.40 lower than the strike and we still have a good deal of time left so this is a real possibility.

What we are doing then is selling 1 contract at the original price of $2 and then selling the second contract at the higher strike price. What would our profits look like then?

If the stock looks like it will be higher than $12.50 at expiration, then anyone that likes this stock would be willing to pay a small premium to prove that it will be $14 at expiration.

This is an Out of the Money call and as such it will be less attractive but it could have a sell price of $1 or more because it has Time Value.

Now let's take a look.

Value of stock 200 x $11.10			-$2,220
Sale of Calls	100 x $2	+$200	
	100 x $1	<u>+$100</u>	
		+$300	
Actual Stock Cost)			-$1920
Income from Stock at Exp.			
Sale (Strike 1)	100 x $10	+$1,000	

Sale   (Strike 2)   100 x $12.50   +$1,250

+$2250

You are selling the stock at two different strike prices—100 shares at $10 and 100 shares at $12.50.

Total Profit   (Income-Actual Cost)   +$330

ROI   (2 Months)   17.1%

You now have a high Return on Investment of over 8.5% a month if the stock ends up over $12.50.

You took advantage of the movement in the stock for a higher ROI

Strategy 4   Wait to Sell Contracts

If we had decided to wait to sell all the contracts at $3 then the ROI would improve to 23.4%:

Cost of stock 200 x $11.10		-$2,220
Income from sale of calls	200 x $3	+$600
Actual Cost of Stock		-$1,620
Sale of stock at Exp.	200 x $10	+$2,000
Total Income		+$2,600
Profit		+$380
ROI (2 Months)		23.4%
		$380/$1620

This is approximately 11.5% per Month

Let's look at these four strategies together and by comparison we can get a feel for the procedures. Remember this is a **two month** call.

	Strategy 1	Strategy 2	Strategy 3 Variation of Strategy 2	Strategy 4
Step 1	Bought 200 $11.10 Price	Bought 200 $11.10 Price	Bought 200 $11.10 Price	Bought 200 $11.10 Price
Step 1A	Sell **2** Call Contracts at $2 Immediately $10 Strike $2 each Rcvd $400	Sell **1** Call Contract at $2 Immediately. $10 Strike $2 each Rcvd $200	Sell **1** Call Contract. Immediately $10 Strike $2 each Rcvd $ 200	No immediate action
Step 2	N/A	Wait 2 Weeks to sell 2nd Contract	**Wait 2 Weeks to sell 2nd contract at higher Strike $12.50**	Wait 2 Weeks to sell both contracts
Step 3	N/A	Sell 2nd Call Contract at $3. $10 Strike $3 each Rcvd $300	Sell 2nd Call Contract at higher Strike. $12.50 Strike $1 each Rcvd $100	Sell 2 Call Contracts. $10 Strike $3 each Rcvd $600
Calls Income	$400	$500	$300	$600
Stock Cost	$2,220	$2,220	$2,220	$2,220
Stock Sale Income	$2,000	$2,000	$2,250	$2,000
Stock Gain (Loss)	($220)	($220)	$30	($220)
Total Gain	$180	$280	$330	$380
Total ROI	9.90%	15.30%	17.10%	23.40%
Monthly ROI		7.60%	8.50%	11.70%

Get a feel for this! The idea is that it is possible to increase your ROI in cases where the stock is showing some real strength. You will get really good at playing this game and it will all depend on how much you pay attention to the fundamentals—News, Experts and Trend. Watch the progress of the stock at all times.

When you get several Market experts all giving a strong buy signal to a stock with a good trend line and positive news, it is a fairly good bet that the stock is going to move positively.

Waiting a few weeks can be a good strategy but it is sensible to stay with Strategy 1 and just enter the Covered Call at the very beginning and not worry about refining the outcome as we did here. These Strategies can be more valuable to you as you gain experience. Even with the fundamentals looking real good there is no guarantee that the stock is going to move in the immediate future, say within a week or two. You will be doing a lot of covered Calls at one time and it may not be prudent to try to refine each one as you go. Obviously if the stock does move in either direction immediately after you purchase then take the appropriate action as outlined.

B. **Strategies Before Expiration**

In most cases we will apply strategy #1 where we simply sell the available contracts immediately after buying the stock. If all goes well then we do not need to take any action.

But what if the stock starts to move against us and it declines in value. There are several approaches that might apply here depending on how quickly and severely the stock decides to dive.

One action would be to buy back the call in the marketplace. This would close out the written call contract, releasing us from our obligation to sell the stock at the call's strike price.

*We must first decide if the buy back cost is appropriate. Closing the call position in this manner, allows us to decide whether to make another option transaction, to hold the stock, or sell the stock. In short the stock is **free of obligations**. If the cost of buying back the call puts us in a losing position it may not be a good strategy.*

Consider the case where the stock goes south after you sell the options. The amount of drop in the market price of the stock and the time remaining to expiration will both determine the cost of the call option. The intrinsic value of the option will be affected immediately but the time value will depend on the remaining time to expiration.

Closing out in this manner frees up the stock so that we can decide if we want to make another option transaction to:

1. Generate income by selling more calls
2. Hold the stock
3. Sell the shares.

It might do well here to note that all *US-listed options that are $0.01 in-the-money, based on the "composite" or "consolidated" closing or last sale price reported by the Options Clearing Corporation (OCC) on the final trading day prior to options expiration, will be automatically exercised.*

This means that you could lose the stock even if the option is only worth one cent at expiration. The stock will be assigned to the call buyer.

Chapter 6

Bringing it All Together

How about a little review. Let's compile a list of the steps that we will take on our journey. Keep in mind that we are dedicated to taking small bites out of the Market and reinvesting to compound our small chunks into big cash.

STEP 1. Go to Granny's house and tell her she is beautiful and that you are her devoted grandchild and—of course she won't believe you but she will love you for being so stupid and give you some money. Kinda ease her thinking into about 2 grand (old guy speak for $2000). All you really need is about $500, but why quibble.

STEP 2. Get your best Geek friend to set up your computer. Remember you need Excel, Internet Access and any fun stuff. Load up your computer with Appendices A & B and become familiar with the various programs that allow you to evaluate returns etc. Get online and look at all the Brokerage houses. Get a tour of the capabilities of each and pick the most flexible and easy to use system. Here are 7 choices that you want to investigate. Each one is unique.

E-Trade	Optionshouse	OptionsXpress
Ameritrade	TradeMonster	
Scottrade	Schwab	

These trading houses have great rates, as low as $4 for stocks. The higher priced houses—about $12 per trade—usually have a much better system in place for normal stock trades and call writing. There are both subtle and obvious differences between these brokers. Some offer services that you might find handy. An example of the differences might be the capability to transfer money from one account to another. With some you can get a next day execution with others it might take a few days. There may or may not be a fee for this service. There may be minimum amounts and also other conditions.

I have had a lot of success with Ameritrade and E-trade, which are full service brokerage houses with strong service and support capabilities. But do your own homework to start and think about using 2 houses when you get a little more skill with this type of trading. The reason for this is to capitalize on the different services offered by each, especially the advice and information sections. Diversification is the key when it comes to listening to advice on a particular stock. You will want to get the opinions of all the experts from both companies to form a stronger base for your stock choices. Additionally, the information will be offered in different styles so that you will grow accustomed to looking at one broker over the other for various types of trades. This will become more apparent as you go!

STEP 3. **Open Your account!**

STEP 4. **Start the fun! Find the stock!**

Remember you are looking for a stock that is priced right for your account, is optionable (market slang for having Options) and has all the good news. Priced right means that you can afford to buy at least 100 shares in order to sell one contract.

Initially you will find it somewhat tedious to search for the right stock since it is not always easy to maneuver the software capabilities of any particular broker. There are some 10,000 stocks in the Market, with a good percentage that are optionable and with a medium price tag of $10-15. This step is the one that you will become the most expert at and you will find that you are using the same stock over and over to produce the cash.

After you have identified several stocks that have all the credentials, go for the best option plan. Do not look to sell options that are further out than two months to start. As you get better you can modify this, but I recommend that you always stay within two months if possible.

This is the crucial step in that options can vary like the seasons and it is wise to look at all cases. When you sell an option you want to get the best deal possible. Remember, if the stock is looking strong it can be smart to purchase the stock and wait a week or so before selling the options in the hope that the stock will move up and provide an opportunity to sell a higher call.

There are some very good charting systems that are capable of selecting stocks from an extremely wide range of criteria such as Price per Share, Price Earnings Ratio, Volatility, Optionable, Trend Charts and a host of very—very useful information including news and advice. They tend to cost on the order of $50-100 per month. I recommend that you make use of some of the cheaper systems on line initially. These systems have the basic capabilities for Covered Call Writing such as options availability, price and trend. Just search the Net for Stock Trading Systems and you will be lead to quite a few.

Your Online Broker can also advise on this matter. After you are proficient at selecting stocks and the associated options you might want look into the more capable systems that are available. I have found Worden Brothers TC 2000 to be an excellent charting system. This system has been operating for a number of years and is extremely sophisticated with its' technical capabilities.

STEP 5. **Calculate the expected Return on Investment.**

We initially set an Return on Investment (ROI) criteria of 3.5% per month. I mentioned once before that you will probably use the same stock several times. A record will be useful when you run out of choices or you simply run out of time, since it will be a ready reference for stocks that have been productive. Using stocks over and over is part of Covered Call Writing.

Keep good records of your transactions. Take a look at the example of Leg 1 transaction in chapter 3. A chart like this will get you started. I am confident that you will expand this to meet your own expectations of a good record.

Read this book several times as you go and after several mistakes you will feel comfortable with Covered Call Writing and I know it will be a good journey for you!!!

Appendix A

Does the Option Fit?

ENTER THE FOLLOWING DATA	Option Period		
	One Month	Two Months	Three Months
Name of Stock	XYZ Corp.	XYZ Corp.	XYZ Corp.
Stock Price	$13	$10	$8
Option Price	$0.10	$0.70	$0.84
Shares Bought	200	200	100
Option Shortfall	**$0.36**	None	None
Req.Option Price	**$0.46**	**$0.70**	**$0.84**
Contracts	**Two**	**Two**	**One**
Req. Investment	$2,600.00	$2,000.00	$800.00
% Income	3.5%	7.0%	10.5%
Required Income	$91.00	$140.00	$84.00
Actual Income	$20	$140	$84
Actual Monthly Percentage	0.77%	3.50%	3.50%
Percentage Shortfall	2.73%		0.00%
Should We Proceed?	**NO**	**YES**	**YES**

Appendix A

Building a 3.5% Chart in Excel

The Index Cell is the Upper Left corner cell and the anchor cell is the Lower Right corner cell. In the Example Output of 3.5% chart the Index Cell is **A1** and the Anchor Cell is **D20**.

This is a 4 (columns) by 20 (rows) matrix and the Index Cell is Blank and the Anchor Cell contains the word NO. Cell A3 is "Name of Stock" and A20 is "Should we Proceed?"

Cells 3,4,5 and 6 in columns B,C and D are your input cells. Row 13, columns B.C and D have fixed percentage inputs of 3.5%, 7.0% and 10.5% respectively.

Rows 7,11,16 and 19 are separators and should be filled Formula cells are in columns B,C and D in rows 8,9,10,12,14,15,17,18 and 20.

After inputting titles in rows and columns input the following formulas:

Cell # B8 = IF(B9<=B5,"None", B9-B5)
Cell #C8 = IF(C9<=C5,"None",C9-C5)
Cell #D8 = IF(D9<=D5,"None",D9-D5)

Notice the pattern. Formulas are similar for each column so cells refer to appropriate columns

Cell#B9 =B14/B6   Cell #C9   =C14/C6   cell #D9   =D14/D6

Cell #B10

=IF(B6=100,"One", (IFB6=200,"Two", (IFB6=300,"Three",
"Contracts?")))

Repeat for #C10 and #D10

Cells B12, C12 and D12   = B6*B4
Cells B14, C14 and D14   =   B13*B12
Cells B15, C15 and D15   =   B6*B5

Cell# B17   =(B15/B12)/1   Cell#C17   =(C15/C12)/2   Cell#D17
=(D15/D12)/3

Format cells for percentage

Cell # B18, C18 and D18   =   IF(3.5%-B17<=0,"", 3.5%-B17)
Cell# B20,C20 and D20   =   IF(B5>=B9, (IFB11="",
                              "Yes", "No")),"No")

Appendix A

Using Chart 3.5 %

After building your Excel program, take some time to play.

Enter different option prices and quantities and check to see if they make sense.

As an example try a stock price of $10 and an option price of $0.35. This should give you a YES in the **Proceed?** Box. This makes sense because the option price is exactly 3.5% of the stock price. Now take a $10 stock price and an option price of $0.34 and you should get a NO in the **Proceed?** Box and the Option Shortfall should show $.01 (one cent).

Try entering 90 in the Shares Bought box and you will get a warning in the Contracts box indicating there is something wrong. Remember you need a multiple of 100 for a contract to be sold.

Appendix B

Power of Compounding

1   Example of compounding 3.5% for Twenty Years

2   Building an Excel Compounding Program

3   Discussion

3.5% Compounding

1.035	Year 1-4	5-8	9-12	13-16	17-20
January	$500	$2,607	$13,591	$70,857	$369,417
February	$518	$2,698	$14,066	$73,337	$382,347
March	$536	$2,792	$14,559	$75,903	$395,729
April	$554	$2,890	$15,068	$78,560	$409,580
May	$574	$2,991	$15,596	$81,310	$423,915
June	$594	$3,096	$16,142	$84,155	$438,752
July	$615	$3,204	$16,707	$87,101	$454,108
August	$636	$3,317	$17,291	$90,149	$470,002
September	$658	$3,433	$17,896	$93,305	$486,452
October	$681	$3,553	$18,523	$96,570	$503,478
November	$705	$3,677	$19,171	$99,950	$521,100
December	$730	$3,806	$19,842	$103,449	$539,338
January	$756	$3,939	$20,537	$107,069	$558,215
February	$782	$4,077	$21,255	$110,817	$577,752
March	$809	$4,220	$21,999	$114,695	$597,974
April	$838	$4,367	$22,769	$118,710	$618,903
May	$867	$4,520	$23,566	$122,864	$640,564
June	$897	$4,678	$24,391	$127,165	$662,984
July	$929	$4,842	$25,245	$131,615	$686,189
August	$961	$5,012	$26,128	$136,222	$710,205
September	$995	$5,187	$27,043	$140,990	$735,062
October	$1,030	$5,369	$27,989	$145,924	$760,790
November	$1,066	$5,556	$28,969	$151,032	$787,417
December	$1,103	$5,751	$29,983	$156,318	$814,977
January	$1,142	$5,952	$31,032	$161,789	$843,501
February	$1,182	$6,160	$32,118	$167,452	$873,023

APPENDIX B

March	$1,223	$6,376	$33,242	$173,312	$903,579
April	$1,266	$6,599	$34,406	$179,378	$935,205
May	$1,310	$6,830	$35,610	$185,657	$967,937
June	$1,356	$7,069	$36,856	$192,154	$1,001,814
July	$1,403	$7,317	$38,146	$198,880	$1,036,878
August	$1,453	$7,573	$39,482	$205,841	$1,073,169
September	$1,503	$7,838	$40,863	$213,045	$1,110,730
October	$1,556	$8,112	$42,294	$220,502	$1,149,605
November	$1,610	$8,396	$43,774	$228,219	$1,189,841
December	$1,667	$8,690	$45,306	$236,207	$1,231,486
January	$1,725	$8,994	$46,892	$244,474	$1,274,588
February	$1,786	$9,309	$48,533	$253,031	$1,319,198
March	$1,848	$9,635	$50,232	$261,887	$1,365,370
April	$1,913	$9,972	$51,990	$271,053	$1,413,158
May	$1,980	$10,321	$53,809	$280,540	$1,462,619
June	$2,049	$10,682	$55,693	$290,359	$1,513,810
July	$2,121	$11,056	$57,642	$300,521	$1,566,794
August	$2,195	$11,443	$59,659	$311,039	$1,621,632
September	$2,272	$11,844	$61,747	$321,926	$1,678,389
October	$2,351	$12,258	$63,909	$333,193	$1,737,132
November	$2,433	$12,687	$66,145	$344,855	$1,797,932
December	$2,519	$13,131	$68,460	$356,925	$1,860,860

Appendix B

Building an Excel Program for Compounding

Refer to the example of Compounding 3.5%.

The Index cell is A1 and the Anchor cell is F49. Building the program is based on simple recalculation on accrued capital.

This program is a 6 column by 49 row matrix.

Follow the format of the example. Cell A1 is where you input your expected monthly percentage and the initial capital will be the input for Cell B2.

A percentage of 2 is input as 1.02, 3.5% is input as 1.035, 4% as 1.04 etc.

In the example, the expected monthly percentage is 3.5% which is input as 1.035 in Cell A1 and the initial capital is $500 which is input in Cell B2.

Insert the formula A1*B2 into Cell B3. This formula is simply the capital invested times the percentage factor and will be repeated for every month of the twenty year program.

Once we set the formula into Cell B3 all we need to do is copy the formula into every cell up to F49 which will be the interest rate times the previous cell of F48.

If we start with a $500 investment and we achieve our goal of 3.5% a month profit then for month two the new investment is $500 plus 3.5% of $500 or $518. This new value of $518 is then reinvested and we now make an additional 3.5% on this value bringing the new value to $536. This is compounding.

Appendix B

The Power of Compounding

After you have built your Excel program you can calculate any combination of starting capital and expected monthly percentage. Enter the proper multiplier in Cell A1 for the monthly percentage desired and the initial starting capital in cell (B2). The multiplier for a 2% monthly profit will simply be 1.02 and 1.035 for 3.5% and 1.05 for 5%. For each year the total $$ accumulation will be calculated based on reinvesting your monthly gains. You can do this for any percentage you choose. Just use the proper multiplier. The results of entering any combination of 2%, 3.5% and 5% with an initial investment of $500, $1000 or $2000 will appear at the end of the last column—Cell F49.

As an example: On January 1st we deposit $500 in our account and we make a trade that gives us 3.5% monthly return. On February 1st we now have $500 x 1.035 or $517.50—rounded to $518. We make another trade and make an additional 3.5%. We reinvested the entire $517.50 so we now have $517.50 x 1.035 or $535.61 at the beginning of March. This is repeated every month and the money is compounded. A twenty year investment of $500 at 3.5% would net you $1,860,860.